Common Problems with the Elderly Confused

AGGRESSION

Graham Stokes
BA, MSc, PhD, ABPsS

Series Editor: Una P Holden

WINSLOW PRESS
Telford Road, Bicester, Oxon OX6 0TS   Telephone (0869) 244644

First published in 1987 by
Winslow Press, Telford Road, Bicester, Oxon OX6 0TS
Reprinted 1987

ISBN 0 86388 055 X

WP153/Printed in Great Britain by Hobbs the Printers Ltd, Southampton

CONTENTS

Dr Graham Stokes is a senior clinical psychologist at Walsgrave Hospital, Coventry, with special responsibility for psychology services to the elderly. He graduated from the University of Leeds in 1976 and obtained his doctorate and qualification in clinical psychology at the University of Birmingham. Since qualifying he has worked in the field of adult mental health and now specialises in the psychological management of the confused elderly.

Discovery

He Used to be so Gentle

Aggression is both frightening and potentially dangerous. Whether it is a physical attack or verbal abuse, to be the victim of such behaviour is always distressing. If a person's outbursts of anger and violence are unpredictable, it is also difficult to feel at ease in their company. There is a constant need to be vigilant and on your guard.

For carers of elderly confused people, it is necessary to be aware that violent outbursts are not confined to the young, fit and able. A sizeable minority of the confused elderly display temper tantrums and aggressive behaviour causing their supporters serious management problems. Not only does decreasing physical strength fail to deter aggressive intent, but acts of hostility are often unexpected and inexplicable. Invariably there appears to be no rational reason for the outburst. Yet why should there be a straightforward and logical explanation for the behaviour, embedded as it is in a confused and partial understanding of events?

However, whilst aggression occurs as a result of a deteriorating memory and a declining ability to reason and exercise judgement on the part of the confused aggressor, outbursts of temper and violence cannot be attributed solely to organic changes within the brain. Whether you are trying to understand an act of physical aggression or an outburst of verbal abuse you cannot divorce the hostile incident from the circumstances within which it took place. Aggressive behaviour rarely occurs without reason. Nor is it the case that aggressive behaviour is closely linked to the severity of intellectual deterioration. Even those elderly confused who are suffering from mild dementia and remain reasonably independent may become abusive and violent.

Family Care

Dedicated and loyal carers who struggle for years with time-consuming demands as their confused relative slowly loses touch with reality and becomes increasingly dependent may react to the appearance of aggression with dismay and bewilderment. Those who are victims of assault or abuse more often experience the attack as emotionally hurtful rather than physically harmful. The painful discovery that someone loved for so many years can behave in such a way can be extremely distressing. There is a desperate need to make sense of the situation, and to know why sudden acts of aggression and violent outbursts of temper now characterise a once considerate and gentle person. Were they always like this beneath the surface and I never realised? Why does he dislike me so? What am I doing wrong?

The torment of such concerns, as well as the risk of injury and damage to possessions, can become an intolerable source of stress. Whilst the problem of aggression is not a constant pressure every hour of every day, and so exhaustion and strain are not to the fore, feelings of inadequacy, apprehension and guilt are commonly felt. Eventually, such feelings may cause a distressing breakdown in the caring relationship and a request for institutional care.

Institutional Care

Around half of the residents of ordinary residential homes are handicapped by confusion and therefore may present with aggressive behaviours. Whilst many homes have a policy of refusing to admit old people who have a history of violence, there remains the problem of those elderly confused who were once placid and cooperative yet unexpectedly become aggressive as time passes.

Often the appearance of aggression is a major reason for admission of an elderly confused person to hospital care. However, the philosophy and design of both residential homes and hospital wards are frequently ill-suited to the demands of controlling violent behaviour.

Residential establishments are often the least well equipped to manage the problem. Untrained staff coping with disoriented and dependent elderly can face seemingly insurmountable crises when confronted with a resident who becomes violent. Staff will not only be concerned for their own safety, but will be anxious about the well-being of other residents, many of whom will be frail and suffering with physical and sensory handicaps. Trained nurses working on busy psychogeriatric wards also need to be prepared for the elderly confused aggressor who vents anger against not only staff but vulnerable patients. The management situation can become especially acute when staff shortages occur.

If the final solution appears to be the isolation or restraint of the aggressor this can confirm the negative image many people have of long-term institutional care. This image is one of punitive management regimes which focus upon the negative features of a person's behaviour to the detriment of individual rights and liberty.

Overall, uncertainty about an appropriate management response and the stress of responsibility can lead to feelings of despair and exasperation among care staff.

When faced with these management difficulties the need for specialist skills to cope with the problem of aggression is essential. The more supporters understand about the reasons for the behaviour and the more able they are to defuse explosive incidents the better equipped they will be to care for potential aggressors. Unfortunately, a common impression is that as memory loss has occurred there is little that can be done either to change or control a confused person's behaviour. Whilst organic changes cannot be reversed, this pessimistic attitude is unwarranted. Although learning is dependent on memory there is nearly always a degree of learning potential remaining. However, as aggression can be a reactive problem in response to the actions of others the issue may often be whether *carers* can learn new habits.

It is the purpose of this book to give practical help to nurses, care staff and relatives on handling some of the difficult situations which arise when confronting the problems of aggression and violent outbursts of temper. There are no magic answers, nor foolproof interventions, but there is plenty of evidence to show that behaviour can change and management mistakes be avoided.

Keyword Summary

Aggression
- Physical attack or verbal abuse
- Unpredictable outbursts
- Hostile incidents cannot be separated from their context

Family care
- Emotional reactions of carers
- Possible breakdown in caring relationship

Institutional care
- Aggression can cause admission to hospital
- Residential institutions unprepared for aggression
- Staff and residents both at risk
- Stress of responsibility

Specialist skills
- The need for understanding
- Improvement is possible
- Can carers learn new habits?
- Practical help for nurses, care staff and relatives

2

Why is it Happening?

In the same way as it is wrong to assume that all old people are alike simply because they are elderly, it is also a mistake just to label a confused person as aggressive and consider that no further investigation is needed. There are many different reasons why an elderly confused person may start to be violent or abusive and each type of aggressive behaviour will require a different response from staff or relatives.

Definition

Aggressive behaviour may occur in the form of:

- an act of physical aggression against a person
- damaging property
- an outburst of temper
- verbal abuse or threats.

It is *not* to be used as a description of mood (eg. when a patient is irritable or cantankerous) or motivation (eg. when a resident is acting stubborn).

Whilst an elderly confused person may be acting out physical or verbal aggression it should not automatically be regarded as evidence of irrational and inappropriate behaviour. Has the person a legitimate complaint? Even though you may consider that the hostile reaction is out of proportion to any possible grievance this is no reason to dismiss the behaviour as not worthy of understanding.

However, understanding aggression is not easy. The confused elderly cannot provide well-argued reasons for their behaviour as the competent aged can more easily do. As a result aggression among the dementing is often described in terms of personality rather than evidence of undesirable behaviour specific, for example, to threatening circumstances. Such an attitude is both a disservice to the person and an unhelpful approach to management. So always be patient and tolerant when investigating the problem. Impatience may lead to the neglect of the confused residents' needs.

However, once you have identified the existence of a socially disruptive problem, it is important that you take action, bearing in mind that the confused themselves are unlikely to be able to explain or recall why they are aggressive.

Possible explanations

Defensive behaviour

Aggression may be a defensive reaction to threatening intrusions of personal space. Assisting an elderly confused person in basic self-care tasks such as dressing or bathing may be resisted because of embarrassment or fear. As memory function progressively fails the non-recognition of carers can seriously aggravate the problem. You know why you are trying to help them in an intimate manner, but to the confused resident or patient you are a stranger whose motives are unknown. As memory loss worsens over time even partners of many years may cease to be familiar and be regarded instead with suspicion.

Failure of competence

Attempts to help the elderly person with everyday activities may be unwelcome as they are explicit evidence of incompetence. It is common for the confused elderly to deny or fail to accept their dependence on others as they hold onto a past which is a record of life lived successfully. Exposing inadequacy may be resented and generate aggressive or abusive behaviour. Similarly, a question and answer session designed to test memory may be met with extreme annoyance and an abrupt termination of the interview.

Disinhibited over-reaction

Frustration is at the root of much aggression. Thwarted desires, obstacles to achievement or an experience of failure may produce frustration-related anger. For an elderly confused person an unexpected change in routine, a misplaced article of value or a name that cannot be recalled may result in frustration and an outburst of temper which is poorly controlled. The target of hostility may be an innocent victim upon whom the aggression is displaced.

Reality confrontation

Exposing an elderly disoriented person to the painfulness of a present which is characterised by a loss of persons, places and things can result in anger as they attempt to seek security and pleasure in a reassuring past.

Alarm

Abrupt and rapid approaches toward a confused person, especially if they come from behind or involve unexpected physical contact can easily result in a hostile act of self-protection. If the elderly person suffers from poor eyesight or impaired hearing the chances of provoking aggression are even greater.

Misunderstanding events

Trying to make sense of a world through a mist of confusion can easily result in misunderstanding and inappropriate reactions. For example, perceiving a community nurse who visits regularly as an uninvited and unwelcome intruder; holding a belief that fellow residents are strangers who are interfering with personal possessions and failing to respect privacy; making the mistake that the home help who is assisting a frail partner to get out of bed is committing a physical assault; or, interpreting the plan for respite care as evidence that people have ganged up to throw them out of their house. Such misunderstandings can understandably be responsible for aggression.

'Adaptive paranoia'

Paranoia (often known as paraphrenia in the elderly) is a mental illness characterised by a morbid suspicion. However, in dementia an 'adaptive paranoid' phase is common. This phase is *not* evidence of a psychotic illness but is a means by which the frightening implications of a deteriorating memory are denied. Making accusations against others to explain why items cannot be found or why an arrangement was forgotten can provide external sources of blame for internally caused errors. As such attempts to hide incompetence are early rather than late features of dementia, the accusations may at first appear plausible.

Manipulation

The elderly confused may use aggression as a means to manipulate carers and fellow residents in order to get their own way. Such behaviour is likely to be maintained by the success of 'bullying'.

Attention-seeking

As a result of the possible disastrous consequences of violent behaviour it is a powerful means of gaining attention. While carers may show disapproval of aggression they are being forced to take more notice of the person and give more of their scarce time.

'Secondary' aggression

Aggression may be the unanticipated reaction to a carer's response to contain or control another disruptive behaviour, such as wandering. Thus, the focus of intervention should not be the aggression but the approach to the original problem behaviour which is experienced as anti-therapeutic.

As you can see, aggression is by no means an easy problem either to understand or resolve.

Keyword Summary

Aggression
- A definition
- Has the person a legitimate grievance?
- Not a personality trait

Possible Explanations
- Defensive behaviour
- Failure of competence
- Disinhibited over-reaction
- Reality confrontation
- Alarm
- Misunderstanding events
- 'Adaptive paranoia'
- Manipulation
- Attention-seeking
- 'Secondary' aggression

3

Making Matters Worse

Whilst changes in memory and judgement are contributing to the problem of aggression this is obviously an incomplete explanation. Behaviour is influenced by the environment, and thus an elderly person can appear seriously deteriorated even though severe brain damage has not occurred, if they happen to live in unsupportive surroundings. This is the great hope for the management of the confused elderly, for whilst you cannot reverse the organic disease, you can provide helpful and compensatory environments. Unfortunately, environments also exist which make matters worse. For example, unsatisfactory living arrangements and unthinking care practices can easily exaggerate the likelihood of violent and abusive behaviour by either failing to prevent the circumstances which give rise to aggressive outbursts or by reacting unwisely to an episode of aggression.

Institutional Settings

Admission to an institutional setting, or a transfer to another ward or unit more able to manage disturbed behaviour is likely to result in a worsening of the problem as the person experiences adjustment difficulties. Hospitals and residential homes are rarely havens of stability and tranquillity characterised as they are by staff changes and a loss of privacy. Entry inevitably involves a break with previous attachments and a disruption of customary routines. Even the loss of a partner who is no longer recognised as a spouse and with whom the confused person has quarrelled and fought for many months may cause upset. The overall experience of disorientation, non-recognition of carers who are preventing a return to familiar surroundings and the close proximity of other confused elderly can easily lead to an unwelcome increase in frustration and fear.

In some homes for the elderly inactive and bored residents spend most of the day sitting down doing nothing with only mealtimes to look forward to. Many of them have been brought together to pass their time in cramped social conditions in small lounges or day rooms that would be frustrating even to younger, well-controlled adults. Violent reactions are therefore understandable.

Whilst the move to group living units has much to commend it, when this has meant that traditional homes have been adapted to allow such a development the resulting living space is frequently confined and inadequately designed. A common example is a juxtaposition of kitchen, dining and lounge areas within the same room. The noise in such units can readily be experienced as an annoying irritant.

When the group-living philosophy extends to sleeping arrangements, the situation can arise where two confused residents who have had no contact throughout the day find themselves sharing a room at night. It is not surprising that they may regard each other with suspicion.

Uniform colour schemes and a lack of information which make it difficult for residents to find their way from one location to another and identify specific rooms can result in disoriented behaviour. If the outcome is a confused person disturbing fellow residents in their bedrooms whilst searching, for example, for the toilet or their own bedroom the prospect of an aggressive confrontation is great.

Care Practices

Despite living so closely with other people, an elderly resident has on average as little as eight minutes' conversation each hour. This takes place normally with other residents for staff normally spend time with residents only when they are 'doing' something for them. Unfortunately, those residents who are the most confused tend to be even less involved and more likely to be ignored. That is, until they start to become difficult or disruptive. Giving excessive attention to a person who is aggressive even if it is born out of a wish to protect other residents can lead to an increase in the unwanted behaviour, especially if this is the only time they are in social contact with the resident. Some old people will do their utmost to gain attention, even though this may consist of disapproval and annoyance.

Whilst it is important to reduce the distress and disturbance of confusion, a rigid adherence to the practice of reality orientation can create more problems than it resolves. The provision of accurate information regarding time, person and building orientation is unlikely to be resisted, but to challenge emotionally sensitive distortions may be less acceptable. A policy of confronting residents with the truth regardless of individual need represents an institutionalised approach to management rather than an enlightened and credible therapeutic response to the problem of disorientation.

Ignoring legitimate complaints which are causing the confused resident displeasure can only generate anger and outbursts of temper. Just because an elderly person is confused does not mean they no longer have an appreciation of personal likes and dislikes. An example of a lack of understanding for individual requirements is when confused residents are expected to retire to bed when routines dictate, and not when they are indicating a wish to do so.

Imposing 'hands-on' activities such as washing, shaving, dressing, etc., not only risks defensive responses, but may unnecessarily challenge the resident's level of competence. The outcome will not only be resentment and anger, but also a less able resident as they are progressively de-skilled. It should also be borne in mind that male residents may not take kindly to a woman dressing or bathing them.

Staff reaction to other unwanted behaviours may also lead to aggressive outbursts. Confronting a wanderer with a demand that they return to the lounge or ignoring the repetitive requests of a confused patient may result in a catastrophic reaction. Even an inappropriate staff response to the problem of incontinence can lead to aggression. If an incontinent resident is allowed to wet, when carers intervene to help change clothes and underwear this invasion of privacy can trigger an aggressive outburst. If an incontinence management programme had been in operation such intimate 'hands on' activity could have been avoided.

The response of care staff who may have little knowledge of how to manage aggressive behaviour in the confused elderly and who are often working under pressure can do more harm than good. If staff are disorganised, uncertain and quite anxious themselves about the situation the confused resident can become even more agitated. Confrontational responses will lead to a spiralling of aggressive intent. Restraints, if they are used, can become objects of hostility and destroy the relationship between carer and aggressor. They invariably increase resistance instead of calming or quieting the confused person.

Large numbers of old people suffer from poor hearing and eyesight. If these handicaps are left unattended there is a greater risk of events being misunderstood and actions being misinterpreted. The likelihood of violent behaviour is therefore increased.

Living at Home

Although the elderly confused often feel more safe, secure and comfortable in their own surroundings such sensations can fail to avert aggressive outbursts. It is believed that there is a greater likelihood of abusive and violent behaviour in institutional settings; however it can also be the case that strangers can inhibit such behaviour due to the continued existence of over-learned social skills. The presence of familiar faces at home can reduce the power of restraining influences and result in increased aggression.

The understandable concern a relative shows for the plight of their confused loved one can on occasions lead to over-protection. Threatening their competence as minor weaknesses are exposed through unnecessary hands-on activities breeds misunderstandings and resentment. Robbing an aged person of their independence is never advisable.

Adhering to standards of behaviour which applied before the onset of confusion will lead to angry confrontation. Expecting a muddled partner to behave as they once did, for them to respect previous standards of politeness, cleanliness and tidiness is unrealistic. You may wish them to be as they once were but to attempt to maintain such ideals will only rouse dissatisfaction and frustration.

Finally, excluding a confused partner or relative from discussions about hospital or social services holiday relief or day care may unfortunately result in misunderstanding, increased confusion and anger. What may have been a sensible response to a demanding situation, may instead be an additional source of tension and disagreement.

Keyword Summary

Behaviour is influenced by the environment

Unsupportive environments

Institutional settings
- Problems of adjustment
- Inactivity and boredom
- Cramped social conditions
- Shared bedrooms
- Disorientation

Care practices
- Ignoring appropriate behaviour
- Giving excessive attention to disruptive behaviour
- Rigid practice of reality orientation
- Ignoring legitimate complaints
- Unnecessary 'hands-on' activity
- Mismanagement of problem behaviours
- Ill-prepared or inappropriate response to aggression
- Sensory handicaps left unattended

Living at home
- Familiarity can reduce inhibition
- Threatening independence
- Unrealistic standards of behaviour
- Exclusion from decision-making

4

Understanding the Individual Problem

Through being well-informed and understanding why residents or patients are behaving as they do, aggression can be prevented. Yet how is this to be achieved given that the confused elderly have difficulty communicating with others?

At one level it is important to recognise that you can describe the reasons for aggressive behaviour in general terms (eg. failure of competence, reality confrontation, manipulation, 'secondary'). However, it has ultimately to be seen as an example of disruptive behaviour *unique* to an *individual*. You therefore need to take into account all the various possibilities which may be leading to the aggression as it is occurring *now*. Do not rely on guesswork or on an opinion based on a previous episode of aggression as outbursts can occur in the same person at different times for different reasons.

What is Causing the Behaviour?

It is misguided to label a confused person as aggressive. Nobody is aggressive the whole time. It is not a continuous activity. People display physical aggression, throw temper tantrums or are abusive in response to somebody or something. Whilst their reasoning or judgement may be defective or bizarre, this does not provide evidence of an aggressive personality.

In order to understand what is responsible for triggering a violent reaction you need to look at the situations in which it occurs. This involves not only identifying when and where the aggression takes place, but also noting what the person was doing before the incident and what the response of carers was to the outburst. This task can be carried out by following the *ABC analysis of behaviour.*

A = Activating event or situation
B = Behaviour (in this case aggression)
C = Consequences

Examples of questions which need to be answered under these headings are:

A
- At what time did the aggression occur?
- When and where did the outburst occur?
- What was the person doing immediately before the aggressive outburst?
- What was the victim doing prior to the incident?
- What was happening around the aggressor at the time?
- Do explosions of rage or physical hostility occur with particular staff or residents, or with everyone?

B
- What form did the aggression take?
- Was the aggressor hitting, kicking, slapping or punching another person?
- Was an object thrown at the victim?

- Was the aggressor causing malicious damage to an object?
- Was the aggressor making threatening gestures?
- Was the confused aggressor verbally abusive or making threats?
- Was the aggressive outburst a temper tantrum?
- Was the person agitated or distressed whilst acting out their aggression?
- Were they saying anything during the aggressive incident?

C
- What was the response of carers to the aggression?
- Was the person comforted; told off; confronted; ignored; sedated; or restrained?
- What was the aggressor's response to the approach of carers to the violent situation?
- What was the reaction of the victim to the attack?
- What was the reaction of other residents?

The ABCs are recorded each time an incident of aggression is observed. All staff should be aware that the behaviour is being monitored. It is best if you record the information at the time of the incident as it is easy to forget the exact circumstances if you leave the recording until later.

As you can see, a Behavioural Analysis provides an accurate and detailed description of actual behaviour in terms of how often it occurred, the circumstances in which it arose and the consequences for the elderly confused aggressor. However, to complete the analysis two additional areas of information need to be obtained.

Background

First, it is essential to record the background to the aggression in order to understand effectively why it occurred. For example, had anything happened during the day (or night) which may have caused upset, annoyance or excitement? Has there been a recent change in routine? Has the elderly person recently moved to new surroundings? Has the aggressor experienced a recent bereavement? Is the elderly person on any medication? Has there been a change in medication? Does the resident appear in pain? Does the aggressor suffer from poor hearing or vision?

Life History

Second, you must also take into account the elderly confused's life history, otherwise their aggressive reactions may be influenced by factors of which you are unaware. Is the aggression being triggered by a denial of long-established rituals and habits? Is the elderly resident finding living with others in a confined space annoying after years of solitary existence? Did the aged person always resent being told what to do? Did they have a reputation for being surly, abusive or having a fiery temper?

The message for professional carers must be 'know your clients'. In order to obtain a comprehensive personal history (eg. previous life-style, habits at home and work, beliefs and expectations, attitudes toward violence, sources of stress, methods of coping with change and stress, etc.), not only do care staff and other workers need to be involved in the process, but so do the family of the confused aggressor.

Recording the Information

The collection of all this information on possible contributory factors can be displayed on a record chart similar to that below (with a covering sheet to provide space for a personal history):

DATE & TIME	A	B	C	BACKGROUND

The Procedure

This first stage in the management of aggression will help identify whether a consistent pattern exists. In order to get a clear picture, the problem behaviour should be monitored for a period of weeks in order to avoid making decisions on the basis of short-term fluctuations in responses. The information obtained should be shared with all carers, mentioned at 'handover' reports and discussed during staff meetings.

If you take time to assess the situation you will avoid the unjust labelling of an elderly confused person as aggressive when they are in truth responding to specific circumstances. Impatience can easily lead to false accusations. So always be patient, open-minded and free of prejudice when investigating the problem.

After the information has been collected and the observation period is over an accurate interpretation is essential because the findings decide the method of solving the problem which is most appropriate to the person and their situation.

Misinterpreting the Problem

Before moving on to the stage of intervention a word of warning. Whilst in most instances aggression is the result of an interaction between environment, personality and the elderly person's memory and intellectual impairment, in a few cases the aggressive behaviour may also be the direct or indirect result of localised brain damage. For example, a condition known as prosopagnosia (ie. an inability to recognise faces by vision alone) can result in sufferers being unable to recognise family and friends, and thus resenting their intimate behaviour toward them. Frontal lobe lesions can result in disinhibited aggression which the person is unable to control. In such patients the emotions appear to run riot. The existence of a subdural haematoma is indicated by a history of falls and episodes of confusion and aggression, and will require a medical opinion. The existence of an aphasia is possible (ie. an impairment of communication). This can generate feelings of frustration as the person struggles to communicate with others, and thereby increases the likelihood of temper and rage.

The existence of such biological damage to the brain is bound to interfere seriously with efforts to manage the problem of aggression if it is not taken into consideration. As a result assessment of the aged aggressor by a neuropsychologist should ideally be included in a thorough behavioural analysis, in order to establish the extent of memory loss and whether the presence of other neuropsychological deficits is contributing to the problem. Such action would avoid the risk of misinterpreting the nature of the aggressive reactions. However, the expertise to undertake a complete neuropsychological assessment is not readily available, so an alternative option is to be aware of the possible existence of focal (ie. concentrated in one place) deficits. If investigation of the aggressor's behaviour suggests that it is not related to general intellectual impairment but may involve other forms of brain damage then request the involvement of a specialist.

Whilst seeking an explanation can be a lengthy process, taking the trouble to understand a person's behaviour can save valuable time later. If you intervene too quickly with inadequate information about the person and their problem this may not only be unhelpful, but is likely to result in the situation assuming crisis proportions.

Therapy is the Art of the Possible

During the observation period staff will have spent a lot of time being especially observant in an effort to establish the reasons for the aggressor's problems. However, when the results of the behavioural analysis are interpreted carers must always take into account whether the circumstances responsible for the aggression are not in turn the result of institutional restrictions, for example, managerial policy, building design, staffing levels, etc. Without changes in the latter, attempts to change the former are likely to fail. It is a waste of time introducing a therapeutic response to prevent aggressive outbursts if it will inevitably flounder on the bedrock of institutional inflexibility. Such a state of affairs can be very demoralising for care staff who wish to improve their client's quality of life.

Remember, the home exists for the benefit of residents. As far as is realistic procedures and policy should be flexible and centred upon the individual's needs. The objective must be to create an environment which maximises the confused elderly's potential for independent functioning. In many cases this will involve the introduction of prosthetic aids to compensate for intellectual and physical deficits which cannot be resolved.

Keyword Summary

- Behaviour unique to an individual
- Taking into account all the possibilities for the aggression
- Not an aggressive personality
- ABC analysis of behaviour
- When and where did the aggression occur?
- What was happening prior to the incident?
- What form did the aggression take?
- What was the response of carers?
- A detailed description of actual behaviour
- Background information
- Life history – involve the family
- Know your clients
- Recording the information
- Finding a pattern – the procedure
- Avoid unjust labelling
- The risk of misinterpretation – the possible existence of focal brain damage
- Neuropsychological assessment
- Assessment is a lengthy process yet saves time in the long run
- The obstacle of institutional restrictions
- Home exists for the benefit of residents
- Maximise independence
- Compensate for disabilities

Prevention

5

Good Care Practice

Prevention is always a wiser policy than allowing a problem to arise and then seeking a cure. Simple provisions and policies can significantly reduce the likelihood of aggression becoming a management headache.

On Admission

Admissions to a residential setting can cause worry and fear. Entry to institutional care in old age can even be a crisis. It requires the ability to adjust to a new set of circumstances very different from those to which the elderly confused will be accustomed at a time when intellectual powers are failing and personal resources are limited.

To minimise the potential for trauma there should be sympathetic preparation for entry and possibly a phased admission. In this way adjustment anxieties are contained. The elderly confused should be welcomed with sensitivity. All care staff who will be involved with the new resident should be aware of their needs and personal history. Escort them around the home so they gain an impression of the layout. Introduce them to other residents.

Social graces remain long after confusion starts and so an exercise in courtesy will be appreciated.

Good admission procedures can prevent the onset of aggressive behaviour at a time of involuntary and stressful changes in lifestyle.

Provision of Care

Be patient and encourage independence in daily life. For as long as possible allow an elderly person to care for him or herself. Offer guidance and support if required, but try to avoid unnecessarily taking over responsibilities.

The elderly should not be hurried as they attempt to maintain independence, and so adequate staffing is obviously needed in order that time can be spent with residents. If you have to intervene be respectful, considerate and never patronising. Do not present yourself as an authority figure who is not prepared to listen.

Provide the elderly confused person with a predictable routine. Ensure there is a place for everything, and everything is in its place. Introduce a memory pad to store important information. Such initiatives will help the elderly resident compensate for a failing memory.

Explain the reason for changes in arrangements or a disruption of routine. Introduce new members of staff. Do not ignore the need for the elderly person to know what is happening around them. Whilst understanding of events will be restricted the gesture will be reassuring. Try to keep the strange and the unexpected to a minimum.

Provide age-appropriate occupation and

activity. Set targets which are realistic and therefore reduce the prospect of failure. Try to construct a social environment which is compatible with their needs. Within reason try to remove obstacles to personal satisfaction. In the final phase of life the confused elderly have many of the same needs as do younger people in other periods of life. They may not be expressed, but, for example, to be able, wanted and respected are relatively enduring wishes. Carers have to be aware that an elderly confused resident is not a shell of somebody who was once a person. Each individual remains a person, albeit a confused one.

Keyword Summary

Prevention is wiser than cure

On admission
- Minimise the potential for trauma
- Preparation for entry
- Take an interest in the new resident
- Introduce them to other residents

Provision of care
- Encourage independence
- Be respectful
- Help the resident compensate for a poor memory
- Keep the strange and unexpected to a minimum
- Provide age-appropriate activity
- Respect the individuality of the confused elderly

⬦6⬦

Reality Orientation (RO)

Aggression may result from misinterpretation and misunderstandings as the confused elderly try to bring meaning to a perplexing and ever-changing world. Reality Orientation (RO) is an educational technique which enables disoriented residents to maintain contact with the present and helps them to function in as normal a manner as possible. Some staff may unknowingly be using this method of communication already.

Time, Place and Person Orientation

The objective of RO is to make sure that *every* staff-resident interaction offers a tie with reality. It is for this reason that this approach is known as 24-hour RO. During a person's waking hours staff present detailed information on time, place and the identities of those around them, as well as a commentary on what is happening. Carers explain all that is strange and do not take anything for granted. There is always a need for staff to be in possession of accurate information.

In conversation with an elderly person who is confused information should be communicated naturally. This can occur while daily activities are being carried out. Remind the person of the time, where they are and who you are. Use touch as a friendly aid to communication. Try to get the confused old person to associate physical contact with warmth and affection and not automatically to equate such gestures with threat and reason for alarm.

Since personal identity is an important feature of somebody's reality always correctly identify the person. Whatever form of address is chosen it should always be used consistently and respect-fully. Initially addressing the confused resident by their correct title (Mr, Mrs or Miss) may help to promote self-worth.

To reduce the distress of confusion be friendly, patient and understanding. If appropriate, reassure them that their fears are groundless.

The provision of orientation information is a gentle, supportive procedure. For example:

Time Orientation
'Mr Davis, it is Tuesday today; that is why the nurse is here. She visits you once a week on a Tuesday.'
Place Orientation
'Mrs Byrne, your bedroom is the second on the right along this corridor. Your name is on the door. Can you see the sign pointing toward the bedrooms?'
Person Orientation
'The gentleman you are sitting next to is Mr Adams. Like you, he is a resident at Crescent House.'

At night quietly talk to those who cannot sleep and reassure them about their whereabouts.

Remind them that it is still night-time. If they are sharing a room remind them of this as well. Despite feeling tired and irritated at having been awakened remember to be tolerant, and speak calmly and slowly.

The most effective way to correct inaccurate and rambling speech is to help the elderly confused realise that their beliefs are mistaken and inappropriate. Be logical and matter-of-fact in your approach, yet always showing both kindness and politeness. 'Match' the level of conversation to the patient's ability to comprehend. Help them discover the existence of errors by asking them to test reality. Do their statements coincide with the evidence? Tactfully disagree with mistakes and misinterpretations. Encourage them to examine their initial responses. If necessary, provide clues or partial information in order to jog their memory.

Your approach must always be non-threatening and supportive. If a correct response is given or observed reward with a smile or a simple sign of approval. However, this is reality orientation *not* reality confrontation, so do not argue. Never pressure a confused resident. If there is already evidence of agitation it is better not to correct the distorted or inaccurate beliefs. In the face of resistance it is foolhardy to persist with unwelcome efforts to achieve awareness of what is likely to be a harsh reality. In certain cases when RO is done to excess it can strip some aged people of the mechanism of denial which they may be using to cope with their situation.

When practising RO you must always be aware of the consequences of challenging a confused person. Why are you doing it? Is it going to cause distress and rage, or relief and satisfaction? Whilst it is easier to dispute impersonal information (eg. 'the dining-room is the yellow door, and it is where your lunch will be served at midday'), correcting emotionally significant statements (eg. 'Alex, there is no reason for you to leave the house now, you retired from work years ago'), demands sensitivity and a knowledge of how the person would react to such a challenge. Challenging emotionally loaded material should only take place when you are confident that it will be favourably received, and there is time available to have a calm and compassionate discussion.

The confused with sensory handicaps have an even greater need for RO. If the problem of damaged hearing and poor eyesight cannot be corrected, compensate for these sensory losses by helping the elderly confused identify reality through the use of all five senses: taste, smell, touch, hearing and vision.

This approach to RO can be supplemented by a formal RO procedure within which current information is conveyed to, and discussed with, a small group of confused elderly of comparable ability. A session would be held once a day for about thirty minutes. The focus of attention is the RO board which contains details of date, place, weather, etc. Participants are encouraged to call each other by their names. Specific topics can be introduced, such as a discussion on social activities, staff routines, etc, in order to help group members retain essential information despite their memory difficulties. The topic which is chosen is not as important as the manner in which it is presented. Whilst it should be an easy, familiar one which is meaningful to the group, it should also lend itself to friendly conversation. Newspapers and magazines are important sources of relevant and time-appropriate information and thus useful material for a group. If members of the group give incorrect answers rather than just saying 'no', the therapist should let them know that you appreciate their attempt and give further clues.

Applied consistently, RO should be effective in resolving some of the problems which arise as a result of memory loss. However, the correction of confusion will always require sound common sense and a sensitivity to the needs of the individual residents. The objective is to improve the quality of life, not to create unhappiness.

Keyword Summary

Reality Orientation (RO)
- Provides a tie with reality
- Time, place and person orientation
- 24-hour therapy
- Consistent presentation of accurate information
- Be friendly, patient and understanding
- Help the confused realise their mistakes
- Be logical and matter-of-fact
- Test reality
- Tactfully disagree with misinterpretations
- If necessary provide clues
- It is *not* reality confrontation
- What will be the consequences of challenging a confused person?
- RO demands sensitivity
- Helping those with sensory handicaps
- Formal RO

⟨7⟩

Changing the Environment

To complement the 'talking' component of RO and heighten awareness of surroundings environmental clues can be introduced into a residential home or ward setting.

Building Familiarisation

To reduce the prospect of a disoriented resident failing to locate a specific route or room, the use of signs, symbols and directional arrows can be very effective in making the environment more familiar. By using prosthetic memory aids the residents are helped to compensate for their declining intellectual powers and avoid the distressing feeling of disorientation. Their adoption also reduces the risk of confrontation as a resident is less likely to get lost and inadvertently wander, for example, into another resident's room.

Signs need to be placed in prominent positions and should be large enough to compensate for impaired eyesight. Use simple messages. Personalise bedroom doors with the resident's name. To help those who have reading difficulties large pictorial signs are often better than just the written word.

Providing pathfinder arrows or a coloured track along the wall is a great help. There is little point just labelling the entrance to rooms if the only time residents are able to identify the location is when they are fortuitously standing outside the door. They will also require the 'pathways' to be sign-posted.

Orientation 'clues' are no different from the directional information we require when entering a building for the first time, yet for the memory-damaged elderly their home environment may unfortunately appear to be a building never before visited and thus they continue to need reminders as to their whereabouts.

Colour coding may also be useful. By associating colours with different rooms residents have an alternative key to the geography of the home.

You can imaginatively combine both colour coding and the use of symbols, and get, for example, the following results:

Room	Door	Directional Arrow	Symbol
Toilet	Blue	Blue	Blue 'T' on a white background
Bathroom	White	White	White 'bath' on a blue background
Dining Room	Yellow	Yellow	Yellow 'knife and fork' on a black background
Coffee Room	Brown	Brown	Brown 'cup and saucer' on a yellow background
Bedroom	Orange	Orange	Orange 'bed' on a black background

There are numerous colour combinations, so you can make your choices blend in with the existing decorations and colour scheme. However, always remember to use clear, bold lettering and bright colours.

However, it is not enough simply to put up signs and symbols and expect the elderly residents to grasp the meaning. They must be taught to find their way about. Regardless of how large-lettered and visible the signposts may be they will have little effect on orientation without training. You can introduce the information to a small number of residents in a RO group. After this presentation in the formal setting staff should accompany confused residents around the home or ward a few times pointing out the environmental cues. Eventually residents should be asked to locate what comes next on the route. For example:

Carer: Mrs Rocastle, this is the first floor and we are standing outside the lift. Can you show me where your bedroom is? (The resident makes a mistake.)

Carer: This is your bedroom. All the bedroom doors are orange. This one has your name on, and as you can see it is the third door on the right. What room is this, Mrs Rocastle?

Mrs Rocastle: My bedroom.

Carer: That's correct; who said you wouldn't remember! Now, can you show me where the bathroom is? You need to follow the white arrows.

It is a good idea to encourage residents to use their own cues also. Get them to notice smells and noises which they can associate with the signs and symbols. This will help them build up a lasting mental map of the home.

Do not walk residents briskly from one location to another. Learning should be at their own pace. The most confused will have the greatest difficulty so teaching must take place regularly in order to increase the chances of learning taking place.

Be patient, speak slowly and use short simple sentences. If residents make errors do not get irritated or critical. If they are successful show pleasure and approval, but never be patronising.

When this period of orientation is over, give regular reminders about the geography of the home in everyday conversations. Although constant repetition may seem boring to you, it is not to the forgetful and confused.

The criticism that the introduction of orientation aids creates an institutional atmosphere is untrue. It is the attitudes of staff which are primarily responsible for such an unhealthy development. To claim that such design features would not be in accord with an aged person's own home ignores the fact that in nearly all cases the confused elderly in residential settings were unable to function in that living arrangement and this was the reason for their admission. If nothing is done to provide a supportive environment which compensates for their intellectual handicaps, in the misguided albeit well-intentioned belief that the 'homely' environment must not be defaced, disoriented residents can be subjected to a dependent and degrading existence. Anyhow, it is certainly not the case that a prosthetic environment is incompatible with the wish to create a domestic, 'homely' atmosphere. It simply requires enthusiasm, imagination and a commitment by staff to provide for the needs of the elderly confused in their care.

At Night

Darkness means that misinterpretations are common. What is familiar during the day can appear mysterious and threatening at night. Fear and fight responses are to be expected unless action is taken to reduce the experience of sensory deprivation which is responsible for the heightened disorientation.

A solution is to install night-lights in the bedroom and areas the elderly person may wish to reach during the night in order that the environment is gently illuminated.

The use of a night light not only helps to reduce disorientation, but it also means that accidents are less likely to happen.

Other changes around the home which can be helpful include hanging curtains made of thick material to block out street light. This not only serves to encourage sleep but prevents ambiguous shadows appearing which make, for example, the lampstand look like a person standing in the corner of the room, a mis-perception which understandably causes alarm. Making sure the bed is comfortable, that the room is neither too hot nor too cold and keeping noise and disruptive routines to a minimum will also help a resident have a peaceful night.

As you can see, changing the surroundings, especially by creating a prosthetic environment which provides sufficient cues to aid memory and orientation, is a valuable option for working with the confused aged.

Keyword Summary

Building familiarisation
- Complements the talking component of RO
- Improves orientation and reduces confrontation
- The use of signs and directional arrows
- Consider location and size
- Colour coding
- Learning the geography of the home
- Effective learning techniques
- Regular reminders
- Orientation aids do not foster institutionalisation
- A prosthetic environment can be 'homely'

At night
- Misinterpretations are common
- Fear and fight responses more likely
- The benefits of night-lights
- Minimise the likelihood of shadows
- Encourage sleep – restructure the surroundings

Management

8

The Aggressive Outburst – Do's and Dont's

In busy residential homes and hospital wards violent outbursts often catch staff off guard. Elderly people, because of frailty, slowness and images we have of kindly grandparents are not expected to act out aggression. However, if they should the speed and strength of the attack can cause great surprise.

Whilst you can do your utmost to prevent the likelihood of aggression occurring nobody is infallible and so management mistakes can be made. In addition some elderly confused residents and patients are notoriously unpredictable and thus prevention is a thankless task. As a result staff require knowledge and skills to manage aggression and thereby reduce the risk of injury to themselves, the aggressor and other residents.

The Management of Aggression

a) What not to do

When a confused elderly person in your care becomes physically violent, abusive or displays a temper tantrum:

- **Do not** be confrontational. Never charge in and demand an explanation.
- **Do not** take personal offence at the assault or accusation. You are dealing with an aged and confused person.
- **Do not** raise your voice.
- **Do not** attempt to lead them away or initiate any other form of physical contact as such actions can easily be misunderstood or resented.
- **Do not** rapidly approach the elderly aggressor.
- **Do not** approach the person from behind.
- **Do not** corner them as this will heighten feelings of threat and alarm.
- **Do not** crowd them by calling for assistance from several members of staff.
- **Do not** provoke the aggressor by 'teasing' or ridiculing them.
- **Do not** attempt to use restraints.
- **Do not** show fear, alarm or anxiety yourself as this can either encourage the aggressor to become more violent or serve to agitate them as they sense you cannot cope with the problem.

If you break these guidelines the chances are you will increase the likelihood of triggering a catastrophic and explosive reaction.

b) Recommended practice

To feel confident in your ability to cope you need to be prepared and know what is expected of you at a time of crisis. The following skills, not all of which will be practised in every aggressive situation, are essential features of effective management:

- Stay calm.
- Respect the aggressor's personal space (this varies from person to person, but at a time of distress a distance of about five feet is a useful estimate). Keep your distance and allow the person to remain in their present position. Overall, give the hostile person plenty of room.
- Provide reassurance that they will not be harmed.
- If appropriate (or possible) ask or direct other residents to draw back and not to interfere.
- Ask the aggressor what is troubling them. Try to identify the reasons for their aggressive behaviour. Seeking an explanation will help determine the correct long-term management response.
- Encourage the aggressor to talk rather than act out their anger.
- Listen to complaints. Be flexible and accepting, not rigid or rejecting.
- Provide alternatives to the behaviour (eg. 'Why don't we sit down together, have a cup of tea and see if we can find out what is wrong?'; 'Let us go and see if what you say is correct', etc), or divert their attention. If their aggression stems from a misinterpretation of events the sensitive practice of RO might be appropriate.

If the confused aggressor's keyworker is available, or if they have a good relationship with another member of staff, it is advisable that they take charge of the situation. The keyworker will have most knowledge of the resident, whilst feelings of fondness will conflict with the urge to be aggressive.

After a while a sympathetic, unemotional, but

also firm reaction will invariably encourage the confused aggressor to calm down and possibly even appear contrite and apologetic. At this point do not talk about the aggressive outburst, but rather engage them in casual conversation away from the site of the incident. Somewhere quiet and private. When you feel the resident has settled the time is right to enquire gently about what happened to make them so angry. Emphasise that you do not consider them to be bad, but that you find their behaviour unacceptable. If reasonable action can be taken to resolve the issue which triggered the aggression then introduce the change. Of course, on many occasions you will not obtain a sensible or reliable explanation and this is why you need to investigate the problem through the ABC analysis of behaviour.

c) The victim who is at serious risk

If the confused aggressor is out of control and risks injuring themselves, or if they are attacking, for example, a defenceless and frail patient, respond quickly and calmly.

No more than two members of staff are needed to approach the person (ideally they should once again be well-informed and familiar to the aggressor). Make sure you have nothing visible which could be potentially harmful to either yourself or the aggressor if it were to be grabbed.

Speak gently, yet in a matter-of-fact manner. Explain that you are going to separate them from their victim. Provide a commentary on your actions to minimise the risk of misunderstandings. Inform them that you cannot allow them to injure either themselves or anybody else. Try to distract them by talking about anything other than the aggressive incident you are trying to defuse.

If the aggressor continues with their violent act as a last resort take hold of their arms. There is no need for any other physical contact. Gently lead the aggressor into a space away from others and comfort them. Show understanding. Try to find out why the incident occurred. If the aggressor remains agitated or does not wish to talk, back away and give them room. A single member of staff can now remain to monitor the resident until they calm down (the other carer can comfort the victim). At intervals suggest alternatives to the present behaviour. If you know your client or patient you will be in tune with their needs and more able to provide attractive options.

Distraction

An effective way to reduce the risk of confrontation is to distract the confused aggressor. The idea is to talk about something other than what is going on. Remain calm and speak in short simple sentences. Your aim is to get them to forget their anger and divert them to another activity. Once again, if you know the person well you should be able to talk about a topic that gains their attention.

By following these guidelines on how to communicate with a perhaps determined confused aggressor, you can avoid a traumatic confrontation at a time when everybody involved is feeling at their most vulnerable.

Keyword Summary

- Aggression often catches staff off guard
- Management mistakes can occur
- Unpredictable assaults
- Staff require knowledge and skills

Management of aggression
- What not to do
- Recommended practice
- The victim who is at serious risk
- Distraction

9

Behavioural Methods

Behavioural management has shown itself to be a powerful means of modifying problem behaviour. This approach to care systematically manipulates the social consequences of the unwanted behaviour in order to reduce the frequency of occurrence. It can be especially useful in managing attention-seeking and manipulative responses.

However, if behavioural management is to be a viable therapeutic strategy it requires the elderly confused resident or patient to have a degree of learning potential. If any learning ability does remain, then this management approach will maximise the chances of behaviour change occurring. Fortunately, it is only in the more serious cases of dementia when memory loss is so advanced that all learning potential is lost. Yet, understandably it is those elderly aggressors who are presenting with a mild impairment of memory function who will be the most suitable candidates for behavioural management.

Behaviour Modification

a) A reward system

In general, the basic idea is to deny the elderly confused person, when it is wise to do so, attention whilst they are engaged in aggressive or abusive outbursts. Even disapproval from staff may be counter-productive. It may actually be rewarding and thereby encourage further aggression. As a result of the worry aggressive behaviour causes it has often been shown that it is the attention from staff which maintains the violence and abuse.

However, by ignoring the aggression there is unfortunately a risk that the behaviour you wish to eradicate may in fact escalate. This has always to be borne in mind. Remember, we are concerned with rage, temper and violence which is being used to manipulate or gain attention. The ABC analysis of behaviour already carried out will have excluded other possible explanations for the hostility. Thus, the aggressor may adopt the attitude of 'you might be able to disregard what I am doing now, but try to ignore this . . .'. Carers therefore need to manipulate the attention they give so that aggression has a negative outcome in so much as the aggressor gains no reward or satisfaction, whilst desirable behaviour brings the attention they seek.

When the aggressor is sitting quietly, or participating in a constructive behaviour, reward them with your time and show pleasure. If they are making a request in a polite or non-aggressive manner listen attentively and approvingly and, if appropriate, respond positively. Make it clear why you are pleased. In this way you are not simply ignoring the aggressor when they act out their hostile intent and hoping the problem will disappear, you are also focusing upon behaviours which are both desirable and beneficial.

As you give praise continue to be aware that you should not treat the elderly person as a child or appear condescending. This may not only serve to annoy but may easily undermine confidence and remind them of their declining competence. When communicating with an elderly person the aim must always be to maintain their self-respect and dignity.

However, this method of control will only work if what is given as a reward is seen by confused residents as rewarding and pleasurable. It is *not* your opinion which is the most important. Whilst the approval and attention of a carer may sometimes be sufficient reward in itself, this is not always so. In this situation you will have to enrich the life of disruptive residents by providing them with small tangible rewards which they can either use or consume. Another option would be to provide the opportunity for activity and outings as a reward.

Whatever type of reward is chosen it must be in addition to what is theirs by right, and should not include activities and privileges which are routinely accessible to all.

Another point to bear in mind is always to consider the relevance of the rewards. If a resident is being rewarded with food it would not be very effective if they had just eaten a meal. Similarly, choosing a reward which is readily available anyway is unlikely to be a potent reinforcer of desired behaviour. It therefore makes sense to have a 'menu' of rewards which can be selected from in order to match the demands of the situation.

An alternative idea would be to involve a resident in a token economy programme (TEP). Following a period of appropriate behaviour or after making a request in a socially acceptable manner the resident would receive tokens to be exchanged at a later time for a range of back-up rewards of differing token value. As you can see, this method enables a person to take advantage of their reinforcement preferences which may change over time.

Any reward should be given immediately. If there is a delay the brain damaged elderly may not remember why they are being rewarded and so aggressive responses will continue. It is a strength of TEPs that the tokens are easily dispensed and can be given immediately after the desired behaviour. This can be a problem for most other material rewards. However, if it is difficult for the elderly person either to understand the significance of the tokens or to remember to exchange them at a later time a TEP is not a reward system to be adopted.

During the initial period of learning the reward is given whenever the desired behaviour occurs in order that the confused resident develops an understanding of the changed consequences of their behaviour. However, when appropriate behaviour has become well established you cannot suddenly withdraw the rewarding consequences as such action is likely to result in the reappearance of the original problem. The answer is to gradually move from a system of constant rewarding to a schedule of occasional reward. If maximum opportunity for learning has initially taken place giving the reward at *random* times does not mean that genuine behaviour change will not occur. In many ways being aware that your behaviour will be rewarded but not knowing when serves to maintain that response. This is how gambling can become such a powerful habit! So a policy of intermittent rewarding can serve to maintain the improvement and thereby result in the achievement of permanent change.

The phasing out of artificial tangible rewards is made easier if you have always combined such rewards with a positive 'natural' response, such as praise and approval. Everybody likes to be liked. We enjoy being well thought of and respected. Yet these social rewards are normally experienced in a haphazard way. People are rewarding or failing to reward each other all the time often without realising it. In behavioural management everyday social reactions are being used in a structured way to help bring about and maintain changes in an elderly confused person. In this way the target behaviours are eventually 'trapped' by the naturally occurring social phenomena which obviously remain as the tangible rewarding consequences are gradually withdrawn.

b) Punishment

i) **Time out** is a technique in which the appearance of undesirable behaviour is followed by the removal of the elderly person to an unrewarding area.

When confronted with an episode of aggression staff may eventually feel that the only solution is to remove the aggressor if only for the sake of other residents. This is known as 'time out'. We are not talking about providing the confused person with the opportunity to 'blow off steam' in private away from the tensions which are easily caused by communal living. 'Time out' is a punishment procedure in so much as the negative consequence of being removed for a predetermined period of seclusion is designed to lead to a reduction in the frequency of future episodes of aggression. However, while in theory this should help reduce the problem, in practice such a response from staff is likely to be an unwise and insensitive strategy.

An elderly confused resident who is already aroused and angry is unlikely to welcome the suggestion that they go to an isolated and unrewarding area. So, unless the resident co-operates with the request, efforts to enforce a removal will inevitably result in an explosion of aggressive and resistive behaviour. Even if you were successful in your efforts to persuade the confused aggressor to enter seclusion, in order for the experience to be meaningful they would have to remain there, albeit for a short period of time. This can create additional problems, for if the elderly person should wish to leave and return, for example, to the lounge, how is this to be achieved? Doors cannot be locked. The chance of confrontation and heightened aggression is clearly great. Such considerations cannot simply be disregarded.

As you can see the use of 'time out' can be disastrous in the management of aggression, and in the minority of cases the risk of injury (to both staff and resident) and abuse can be great. Overall, this technique is not recommended.

ii) Response-cost punishment is a procedure in which a person who acts inappropriately is punished by the loss of a previously available reward.

Having discussed with the confused resident what it is they find enjoyable and rewarding, their daily life is enriched through the provision of this reward on a regular basis, say on the hour or at a predetermined time during the day. Select a starting day, and from the moment the day staff come on duty the resident receives the reward at the appropriate times. However, if there is an aggressive or abusive incident the time of the outburst is noted, the resident is informed that the incident has been recorded, and the availability of the reward is withdrawn. This procedure is carried out in a neutral way. To regain the reward the resident must refrain from exhibiting aggression for a set period of time (eg. one hour). If during this 'earning' period they are aggressive again, the one hour penalty recommences from the time of the latest incident (which as before is recorded, and the resident informed). In this way the confused person learns that aggression means that access to a reward is lost, whilst appropriate behaviour ensures the continuation of their enriched circumstances. To avoid boredom, establishing a 'menu' of rewards can once again be useful.

The following case example illustrates the procedure:

Target Behaviour
Temper tantrum (ie. screaming, shouting verbal abuse, shouting demands or requests, throwing objects, banging, collapsing on the floor).

Reward

The use of the record player (to be played at a reasonable volume as defined by nursing staff) for ten minutes on the hour.

Method

- Tell the patient that from now on if he refrains from aggressive behaviour he will be allowed to use the record player for ten minutes on the hour.
- If this goal is achieved go up to him and say 'I'm glad you have been able to control yourself', and direct him to the record player.
- If the patient throws a temper tantrum the privilege is removed. It can be earned back with two hours of 'good' behaviour timed from the end of the outburst.
- If the patient is aggressive during the reward period, access to the record player is immediately terminated.
- When the privilege has been lost it is possible that the patient might try to gain compensation by seeking more attention from staff. Keep attention to a minimum. Be pleasant, but walk away as soon as possible. Do not engage in any 'special activities'. When the reward has been re-earned respond more enthusiastically to his approaches and involve him in activities.

iii) **Conclusion** While response-cost punishment procedures do not create the same problems as time out, as a matter of routine the development of punishment programmes with a handicapped population is difficult to justify. Furthermore, there is something irrational about using punishment to control aggression, for the frustration this will generate is a known trigger of violent behaviour.

Thus punishment would appear to be more likely to encourage aggression than control it.

Overall, rewarding appropriate response is by far the best policy to adopt. Aggression is not a continuous activity so there is always opportunity to attend to and encourage appropriate non-violent behaviour.

General Principles

a) Consistency

It is essential that behavioural management operates as far as is possible for twenty-four hours a day, seven days a week. All care staff must be involved in order to guarantee that the resident is treated consistently, for consistency is the key to success. To ensure a consistent approach the target behaviour, that is the one you are trying to change, must in all cases be accurately defined in advance and be known to all carers.

b) Fading

If behaviour change has occurred within the residential setting or on the hospital ward it is important that the improvement transfers to other environments. This is especially so if the problem has been controlled during respite care or during attendance at a day centre, and you wish for similar success at home where the carer is likely to be under great stress. The technique to adopt is known as fading. In general terms this involves taking a behaviour that occurs in one situation (eg. a hospital setting) and getting it to occur in a second situation (eg. home), by gradually changing the first situation into the second.

While behaviours acquired in a restricted environment such as a hospital usually generalise, to some degree, to other settings, there is the risk that putting a person directly into another environment may result in the loss of the new pattern of behaviour and bring about, in this case, the re-occurrence of aggressive responses. To encourage carry-over it is preferable gradually to move away from the style of management provided, for example, in the hospital and introduce conditions which approximate to those to be found in the home environment. This process can be helped if you can gain the cooperation of relatives so they learn the ways care staff have used to manage the aggressive behaviour. They can then introduce the same techniques of behavioural management into the home, thereby giving rise to a positive similarity across settings. However, a carer should always be reminded of the risk of escalation if they ignore their loved one's aggressive or abusive out-bursts. If this was to happen relatives might have little choice but to give in and accept they are being manipulated. If the caring partner continued to be at risk serious thought would eventually have to be given to the merits of continuing the existing living arrangement.

c) Goal setting

Finally, and possibly most importantly, before you embark upon behavioural management you must be confident that the elderly confused person will be able to benefit from the procedures. What is required is to match the target being planned for the resident with their remaining intellectual ability. In other words the goal must be both realistic and attainable. The memory loss should not be so severe that the goal will always remain incomprehensible and perplexing. To ensure this does not happen keep a record of performance and ensure that a regular review of progress by all carers takes place. The plan of management can never afford to be inflexible. It has to change to meet the changing circumstances that can arise once it has been put into action. In the management of aggression more than with any other disruptive problem there is a possibility of unexpected or even undesirable reactions as the aggressor attempts to outwit the care regime.

The area of behavioural management is one of great complexity even though on a simplistic level it is often understood to be nothing more than a technique to reward good behaviour and punish (or ignore) bad behaviour. Nor is it a mechanistic technology which rejects the need for warm and affectionate staff/client relationships. It is clearly much more than these naive assumptions, so if you feel you require an expert opinion before introducing this method of management seek the help of a clinical psychologist who is skilled in methods of behavioural change.

Keyword Summary

Behavioural management
- Changing the social consequences
- Useful in managing attention-seeking and manipulative behaviours
- Requires learning potential

Behaviour modification

a) A reward system
- When to give attention
- Disapproval can be counter-productive
- Ignoring aggression – the risk of escalation
- Reward appropriate behaviour
- Maintain self-respect
- Find rewards that please – social or material
- A policy of enrichment
- Relevance of rewards
- Token Economy Programmes (TEPs)
- Reward immediately
- Rewards cannot be suddenly withdrawn
- Intermittent rewarding
- 'Natural' social reinforcers
- Target behaviour is 'trapped'

b) Punishment
- Time out
  - removing the confused aggressor to an unrewarding area
  - an unwise and insensitive strategy
  - can lead to heightened aggression
  - risk of injury and abuse
- Response-cost punishment
  - loss of a previously available reward
  - reward regained following a period of appropriate behaviour
  - a 'menu' of rewards

- Conclusion
  - punishment programmes are not recommended
  - punishment = frustration = hostility

General principles
- Consistency – the key to success
- Fading – a similarity across settings
- Goal setting – set realistic targets
  - record-keeping and regular reviews
- Behavioural management is complex
- If necessary, seek an expert opinion from a clinical psychologist

The Supporters

10

Helpful Attitudes

Be Positive

Positive staff attitudes are the key to the success of most of the ideas discussed in this book. It does not matter how effective these methods appear in theory: if the attitudes of those who are putting them into practice are unhelpful they are destined to fail. Lack of interest in the client group or a belief that efforts to improve the situation are pointless are clearly counter-productive. Remember, attitudes influence the way you behave. For example, if things frequently go wrong between you and a resident, are you holding negative opinions which are causing the difficulty? Be tolerant, patient and tactful. Continue to respect the individual. Do not over-react or feel overwhelmed by having responsibility for a resident who is aggressive.

Without being too optimistic have positive expectations. Time and time again the behaviour of the elderly confused improves when thoughtful management is introduced. This involves not only caring for their physical welfare, but also paying attention to their emotional and social needs as well. Do not impose any negative attitudes you might hold onto them. Encourage them to do things and give them confidence to make use of their remaining skills.

Try not to be rigid in your beliefs, and if necessary, re-adjust your attitudes and expectations. If new care techniques are recommended do not automatically regard it as a criticism of what may have been accepted previously as good management.

The Whole Person

Aggression is not simply a problem to be managed. It is a personal difficulty the elderly resident requires help to control. Consider the whole person. Do not selectively attend to the negative features of their behaviour. Whilst they may have an unwanted behaviour, include this in an appreciation of the person who has feelings and preferences and who may be feeling resentful or bitter about their present circumstances. It is naive to assume that an elderly person can easily adjust to failing powers and unwelcome change. Even though confusion may be a barrier to communication and thus make it difficult to appreciate how experiences have shaped an elderly person's life, taking an interest in the whole individual helps you to understand the aged resident better. This must inevitably lead to an improvement in the quality of care you provide.

Burn-out

When many confused people are gathered together problems can appear insurmountable. To manage one aggressive resident may be difficult; to care for several can appear impossible. The risk of confrontations, physical assaults and personal injury can exercise a draining effect on your coping resources.

You may approach your work with enthusiasm, yet soon become dismayed and discouraged by the physical demands, unsocial hours and inadequate support you have to tolerate. It is frequently forgotten that staff require praise and encouragement. It is unrealistic to expect staff to show initiative and enthusiasm if they do not receive the respect and regard their work deserves.

In these situations you need to share your anger, disappointment and grievances. If you do not, you risk experiencing 'burn-out'—feelings of frustration, exhaustion, demoralisation and hopelessness. So, as a regular practice, seek the mutual support of colleagues. Hold group meetings to exchange experiences and concerns. Do not feel embarrassed to acknowledge your doubts and weaknesses, for you will also undoubtedly have assets and strengths your fellow carers may benefit from.

However, if you work in relative isolation and there is little chance of assistance from other carers, try to develop coping attitudes. Dismiss negative and self-defeating ideas. Try to emotionally distance yourself from your problem. Check whether your worries are largely unfounded or exaggerated. Ask yourself whether there is any evidence to support your fears. Do not let your mind run riot to an extent where you cannot 'see the wood for the trees'. Abandon 'what if . . .' thoughts. Try to get things in perspective. Reduce the pressure you feel by avoiding such ideas as 'I should be doing this' or 'I mustn't do that'. Such thoughts increase the demands you place on yourself and make caring even more tiring. Never focus on your feelings of anxiety. Instead, be constructive and concentrate on the task at hand. The demands and pressures may appear endless but you will only successfully get on top of them if you tackle one problem at a time. Positive thinking can help prevent undesirable levels of stress and strain.

Overall, adopting the right attitudes can make you a more effective carer, and as a result help the elderly confused obtain a better quality of life.

Keyword Summary

Attitudes
- Be positive
- Attitudes influence behaviour
- Respect the residents
- Do not over-react
- Remain confident that improvement will occur
- Provide for physical, social and emotional needs
- Do not feel threatened by 'new' ideas

The whole person
- Treat the resident as a person, not simply as a problem
- Take an interest in the whole person – appreciate needs and feelings
- Confusion is a barrier to communication

Burn-out
- Problems appear insurmountable
- Enthusiasm replaced by dismay
- Staff need praise and encouragement
- Burn-out – feelings of exhaustion and frustration
- The need for the support of colleagues
- Coping attitudes – dismiss negative ideas
- Keep things in perspective
- Be constructive – tackle one problem at a time

11

Being the 'Therapist'

Not Just a Carer

As should be clear by now, the effective management of aggression is not something which can be switched on and off. It needs to be practised day in day out. Such a demand for a '24-hour therapy' inevitably involves nurses and residential workers.

The routine work of care staff in daily contact and *communication* with the elderly person means they have a major impact on management. Actually trying to communicate with the confused person is important. Silent care is bad care. You need to move away from the idea that you simply dispense treatment. Instead you talk and listen, explore and investigate, always trying to overcome the barrier of confusion. And it is only those carers who work closely with the person who have the opportunity to do this. Only you can identify the most likely explanations and possible solutions to their problems. The more familiar you and your colleagues are with the elderly resident the more accurate your knowledge will be. Nobody else can possibly be so well informed. No other professional can appreciate the difficulties that arise from day to day. In practice you therefore cease to be simply a carer and become a skilled 'therapist' in your own right.

Medication

Hand-in-hand with an increase in the 'therapeutic' role of carers is the view that the appearance of aggression and abusive behaviour should not automatically suggest that tranquillisers are immediately required. Do not rely on medication to solve the problem. Whilst sedation may reduce the level of aggression, the possible side- and after-effects mean it should be used very sparingly and be an intervention of last resort. When drugs are prescribed their effect on both the elderly person's psychological and physical well-being must be carefully monitored.

Overall, while medication can be helpful, it is an inadequate substitute for patience, understanding and a management regime which satisfies the needs of the elderly confused in care. The use of drugs should always be coupled with 'therapy', and never regarded as a suitable replacement.

Strategy

Below are suggested guidelines for all therapeutic supporters:

- Identify the reason for the aggressive behaviour.
- Make a plan to introduce change. Whenever possible involve the resident.
- Put the plan into action.

- Evaluate the extent to which the plan is effective. Monitor the effect the intervention is also having on the aged person's overall performance and welfare.

Such an approach is not only likely to reduce the burden of responsibility but will also improve your own skills and increase the satisfaction you get from your job.

Keyword Summary

More than a carer
- Good management practice cannot be switched on and off
- 24-hour therapy
- Effective management requires accurate information
- Nurses and care-staff are the best informed
- Being a skilled 'therapist'

Medication
- Do not rely on tranquillisers
- Possible side- and after-effects
- Drugs – a poor substitute for patience and understanding
- Should always be coupled with 'therapy'

Therapeutic strategy
- Find the cause
- Design a treatment plan
- Put plan into operation
- Evaluate the outcome

12

Managing the Problem at Home

There are about 500,000 confused elderly people in Britain, yet less than a quarter of them are looked after in hospitals or residential homes. This means, without any doubt, the family is the main provider of care. Typically, the responsibility is with a partner, daughter or daughter-in-law. Yet relatives struggling to cope with behaviour often as difficult as that found in institutional settings are frequently the forgotten sufferers. This is an intolerable state of affairs. It is not an easy job looking after elderly people who are confused. Relatives need, and should have, outside support.

Although nobody outside the situation really knows what it is like to live with an elderly confused relative who has distressingly become aggressive, it is hoped that many of the ideas described in this book will make the task of caring easier. To end this practical guide here are a few more points to help relatives cope with their unenviable situation.

The Future

Aggression in the confused elderly is not the same as aggression displayed by those people who have their abilities intact and their judgement unimpaired. Try to approach the problem dispassionately. How is the aggression having an impact on your daily life? Whilst verbal abuse is unattractive, it is not as destructive as acting out physical aggression. If a confused person cannot dispel their anger all that remains for them to do if they are to gain some relief from their frustration is to curse those who are nearby. However, if no harm is done (remember, do not take it personally), ask yourself whether you need do anything at all. Sometimes it is best to leave the behaviour alone and accept the situation. If you can live with your relative's tantrums and abuse then you may look to the future with a degree of optimism for there is a good chance this will always be the case. Aggression does not inevitably worsen over time. In many ways as the elderly person's intellect deteriorates they will become more sedentary and passive. Nor does the appearance of aggression mean that other disruptive behaviours will eventually appear.

Coping with Feelings

It is so easy to have bad and upsetting feelings when caring for someone who is regularly aggressive. Do not worry as it is both understandable and natural.

Caring relatives can find it hard to adjust to accusations especially if they are repeated outside the home. Whilst the more extreme accusations (eg. 'my husband has stolen my dentures') are easily dismissed, others may be easier for people to believe (eg. 'they never come to visit me'). As accusations are more common when a person shows limited evidence of incompetence their complaints appear not only plausible, but in the eyes of carers may be seen as deliberately malicious. To be angry is therefore a common response. Try to be angry with the behaviour and not the person. Remember it is a means by which a frightening loss of memory can be denied to both the sufferer and others. Yet, in time, as the awareness of mistakes and errors is eventually lost the 'paranoid' behaviour will also disappear.

Showing nothing more than concern for the confused person's welfare may unfortunately result in verbal or physical abuse. If you try to assert yourself to compensate for their damaged skills or lack of judgement there can be a traumatic clash of wills. Yet all you are doing is expressing your affection after many years of being together. The confusion and upset this causes the loving supporter can be great. It is therefore understandable that many supporters feel they are in a bleak, dark tunnel with seemingly no end.

Although you might feel embarrassed nothing will be gained by keeping the problem a secret from family and friends. Do not be ashamed to share your feelings. Do not cover up because you believe you will be forced to surrender your loved one if others realise the extent of the problem. Whilst your family might be concerned and pressurise you to take a particular course of action, professional workers will allow you to proceed at your own pace so long as you are honest and are prepared to listen to their advice.

It is understandable to grieve for the loss of companionship as a major personality change occurs in those you love. The confused relative who is aggressive can appear even less like the person who was once known and loved. Your relationship may no longer be mutually rewarding. You may understandably become alienated from them as they continue to abuse you for no reason.

You may also be angry with fate having been so unkind. You may be resentful with other members of the family who are not 'pulling their weight'. If you are unable to contain your discontent, you obviously need to do something. At the very least share your unhappiness and possibly even bitterness with those who can relieve your burden.

Some carers can become so enmeshed in their situation that life can appear a never-ending round of supervision and responsibility. Do not take your devotion to extreme proportions. If you are under stress listen to advice from others who are not so closely involved. They might have a more accurate appreciation of the situation.

Some carers benefit from placing an emotional distance between themselves and their caring responsibilities. On occasions some also require a physical distance. If this is how you feel, try to get out, do things, meet people and generally have a break from what may at times be an upsetting and demanding routine. A change of scenery may help you gain a new outlook on your problems. Why not seek the companionship of a Relative Support Group? Groups are springing up throughout the country and so it is increasingly likely there will be one near you. Contact the Citizens Advice Bureau for information or talk to your GP. The benefits of attendance can be enormous. You can exchange practical ideas on how to cope and in general receive mutual help and moral support.

Resources

Do not be reluctant to seek professional help. Contact your GP or local Social Services office to request practical support.

The Citizens Advice Bureau may also have useful tips about local facilities and support services. If you want information about the nature of the problem you are dealing with, there are voluntary organisations such as the Alzheimer's Disease Society which are only too willing to provide guidance. It is often the case that receiving an explanation can give great relief.

You must always consider your own needs if you are going to provide good care. Increasing the resources available to you can reduce the cost of caring and ensure that you are able to continue in your supporting role. Encourage other family members to help you share the responsibility. Do any relatives live close at hand? Could they occasionally come over and keep a watchful eye while you have a day or evening out?

Finally, never feel guilty about no longer being able to be the sole care giver, or your inability to manage without help. These are irrational and self-destructive beliefs. Nobody expects you to be either superhuman or a martyr.

Practical Suggestions

Relatives often complain that they do not receive practical guidance on how best to cope with their loved one's confusion. Yet this can so easily be provided in a straightforward way.

In the home, as in a residential setting,

prevention is a better management strategy than trying to think of ways to cope with aggression while it is taking place.

Work at trying to improve your loved one's memory in order to avoid unjustified accusations or frustration-based hostility. For example, always remember that simple, predictable and familiar routines help reduce the likelihood of confused behaviour. Make sure there is easy access to every-day information.

For example, put up a 'memory board' in the kitchen or any other prominent place. Make sure you include information on the day's activities and especially details of your movements and whereabouts. This is essential if you plan to go out for this will help reduce the risk of misunderstandings arising. Try to make your absence from home predictable. When left alone, your loved one should always have something to do to occupy their mind.

If the elderly person wears a watch, make sure it is accurate. If they are fit and able, encourage them to do chores around the house. This will not only give them interest but will maintain their sense of competence. If confidence can be gained from being involved in the domestic routine your relative is less likely to feel vulnerable and inadequate.

Although aggressive behaviour can make life particularly difficult for supporting relatives, always remain confident that improvement may occur. Use the information in this book to open your mind to ideas and practical suggestions which you may never have considered. It may enable you to make the best of what must often seem an impossible situation.

Keyword Summary

The forgotten sufferers
- The family is the main provider of care

The future
- Some aggression may be tolerable, and may decrease in time

Coping with feelings
- The pain of being accused
- Anger is a natural reaction
- Be angry at the behaviour
- A clash of wills
- Do not be ashamed of your feelings
- Do not keep the problem a secret
- Grief is understandable
- Seek the company of a Relative Support Group
- Emotional distance can be helpful
- Listen to the advice of others who are less involved
- Take a break

Resources
- Seek professional help
- Citizens Advice Bureau may have useful information
- Voluntary organisations
- Recruit family members to help out
- Needing help – do not feel guilty
- You are not superhuman
- Do not be a martyr

Practical suggestions
- A policy of prevention
- Simple and predictable routines are helpful
- Memory board
- Make absences from home predictable
- Clocks and watches – are they accurate?
- Promote independence
- Going out – provide occupation
- Open your mind to ideas

◇

Appendix I

Useful Organisations

Age Concern England, Bernard Sunley House, Pitcairn Road, Mitcham, Surrey CR4 3LL

Age Concern Scotland, 54A Fountainbridge, Edinburgh EH3 9PT

Age Concern Wales, 1 Park Grove, Cardiff CF1 3BJ

Alzheimer's Disease Society, 158/160 Balham High Road, London SW12 9BN

Alzheimer's Scotland, 33 Castle Street, Edinburgh EH2 3DN

Carers National Association, 29 Chilworth Mews, London W2 3RG

Coventry Association for the Carers of the Elderly Confused, Newfield Lodge Day Centre, Kingfield Road, Coventry CV1 4DW

Disabled Living Foundation, 380–384 Harrow Road, London W9 2HU

Help the Aged, 16–18 St James's Walk, London EC1R 0BE

Appendix II
Further Reading for Carers

Forgetfulness in Elderly Persons—Advice for Carers, Age Concern.

Coping with Caring—A Guide to Identifying and Supporting an Elderly Person with Dementia, Brian Lodge, MIND, 1981.

24-Hour Approach to the Problem of Confusion in Elderly People, Una Holden et al, Winslow Press, Bicester, 1980.

Our Elders, G. K. Wilcock & J. A. Muir Gray, Oxford University Press, 1981.

Coping with Ageing Parents, C. J. Gilleard & G. Watt, MacDonald Ltd., Loanhead, Midlothian, 1983.

Thinking It Through, U. Holden, Winslow Press, Bicester, 1984.

Caring for the Person with Dementia, Alzheimer's Disease Society, 1984.

Living with Dementia, C. J. Gilleard, Croom Helm Ltd, Beckenham, Kent, 1984.

The 36-Hour Day, N. L. Mace & P. V. Rabins, Hodder & Stoughton, London, 1985.

Reality Orientation: Principles & Practice, L. Rimmer, Winslow Press, Bicester, 1982.